Jack The Poet

Published by the Langley Press

© 2017 Simon Webb. The right of Simon Webb to be identified as the Author of the Work has been asserted by him in accordance with the Copyright, Designs and Patents Act 1988. All rights reserved.

All pictures in the text are from Everard Meynell's 1913 biography of Francis Thompson and are reprinted by kind permission of
Durham County Council

Jack The Poet

Was Francis Thompson Jack the Ripper?

Simon Webb

Also from the Langley Press

American Jack: Jack the Ripper and the United States

Severin: A Tale of Jack the Ripper

Mary Ann Cotton: Victorian Serial Killer

for free downloads and more from the Langley Press, please visit our website at:

http://tinyurl.com/lpdirect

Contents

1. Among the Dead   7
2. Childhood of a Monster?   16
3. The Outcast   33
4. The Land of the Bare Shank-Bone   43
5. Merry England   54
6. Possibilities   63
7. Blood and Brain   74

Francis Thompson

1. Among the Dead

Some time in the summer of 1887 a derelict medical-school drop-out called Francis Thompson attempted to kill himself by taking two large doses of laudanum.

Exactly where this happened is unclear: some say Thompson planned to end his life in an obscure street near Covent Garden; others that he managed to sneak into one of the London cemeteries to join with the dead and become one of them.

Laudanum, also called opium tincture, is usually a liquid consisting of opium mixed with alcohol. It is still used for medicinal purposes, but in modern times access to it is heavily restricted. By contrast, in Victorian London, laudanum could be bought as easily as aspirin can be bought today. One did not even need to go into a pharmacy to buy this popular narcotic, which was the drug of choice for the Romantic poet Samuel Taylor Coleridge, among others. Laudanum was sold in grocer's shops when the future acclaimed poet Francis Thompson was haunting the capital. Because the drug was regarded as a medicine, it was not taxed in the way alcoholic drinks were and are in England, so that for many Victorians it was a cheap alternative to the more conventional alcoholic drinks that can still be bought today. In the nineteenth century laudanum appeared as an ingredient in many different patent medicines, some designed to treat specific complaints for which even a modern over-the-counter pain-killer would not seem to be indicated.

Like many preparations that include opiates, laudanum, which was invented by the sixteenth-century alchemist Paracelsus, has different effects on different people, and at different doses. Users build up a tolerance for it, so that what might be a regular dose for an experienced addict would kill someone with little or no experience of the drug, or send them into a coma. The novelist Wilkie Collins, who died in 1889, the year after the year of Jack the Ripper, took such large regular doses that when one of his servants tried to take a comparable amount he died almost immediately.

Generally, a big enough dose will induce a state of extreme relaxation, where the opium user becomes inactive, even stupefied, unresponsive to stimulus, and insensitive to what is happening, has happened or will happen in the world beyond his opium haze. Opium is a powerful pain-killer: this means that any bodily aches and pains the opium user has may vanish, or be pushed to the fringes of his consciousness, along with stress, anxiety and other forms of mental pain.

All this sounds very pleasant, superficially, and a similar state could be attained after an excellent dinner, prefaced by a good dry sherry, with a different wine to accompany every chapter or course, and plenty of port as an afterword. Such a meal would probably leave the diner with a strong desire to doze off by the fire, as the last plates are being cleared away, and indeed laudanum can induce sleep: in his celebrated Victorian-set novel

The French Lieutenant's Woman, John Fowles describes an elderly lady who relies on opium to get to sleep, and who suffers from many of the drawbacks associated with opiates, including vivid, disturbing dreams.

Regular users had to increase their dosage to achieve the same effect, and could eventually become dependent on laudanum just to function normally. The aforementioned Wilkie Collins got into a huge panic when he ran out of laudanum during a trip to Switzerland, where its sale was more strictly controlled than it was in England.

Collins also experienced the hallucinations heavy use could bring to laudanum drinkers, which appeared when elements from the vivid opium-induced dreams he experienced when asleep began to intrude into his daytime consciousness. He would see ghosts, including a green-skinned woman with tusks, milling around, and sometimes trying to push him downstairs. He also saw a phantom version of himself, who would try to take over his ink-bottle and writing-paper when he, the 'real' Collins, was trying to work.

Collins's hallucinations are a reminder of the paradoxical operation of laudanum on some people: it seems to stimulate the imagination, while simultaneously suppressing pain, anxiety and wakefulness. In the 2001 Jack the Ripper film *From Hell* a heavily fictionalised version of the real-life police detective Frederick Abberline, played by the American actor Johnny Depp, uses opium mixed with absinthe to induce visions containing clues to the identity of the Ripper.

Although suicide by laudanum may seem like an outlandish thing for the future poet and Ripper suspect Francis Thompson to attempt on that summer night in 1887, this particular pathway to oblivion was well-worn in Victorian times. Although the Christian Church featured more largely in many people's lives than it does now, and suicide is regarded as a terrible sin by many Christians, the desperate circumstances of many people who lived in London when Thompson was existing as a homeless derelict there tempted them to end their lives, which many had been forced to live quite without hope. Reflecting the Churches' line on suicide, suicide itself was illegal in nineteenth century England, and people who attempted to kill themselves, and failed, could be arrested.

In 1891, after he was discovered as a writer and lifted, by a seeming miracle, out of utter destitution, Francis Thompson wrote a review of an important book by General William Booth, founder of the Salvation Army. This was *In Darkest England and the Way Out*, first published in 1890, in which Booth draws on personal observation, statistics, and reports from fellow Salvationists to build up a terrifying picture of life for the poor in Victorian London and, to some extent, in other parts of Britain.

The General begins his book with a reminder of the adventures of the explorer Henry Morton Stanley in the jungles of 'darkest Africa': the author compares the natives of these vast forests to English people forced to live in the country's most notorious urban slums. Like the Africans of the jungle, these people know nothing but their apparently inescapable surroundings, and they must be shown 'the way out'.

Booth reports that over four hundred people a year were arrested for having planned or attempted suicide in London, and he gives a detailed and harrowing true account of a 'respectable' Holloway chemist and his wife who were driven to attempt suicide by sheer starvation and exhaustion.

The plan was that Arthur, the chemist, and his wife would cut their own throats, having first given strychnine to their son, an only child nicknamed Arty. In a letter read out in court during the couple's trial for attempted murder, Arthur stated that 'We have, God forgive us, taken our darling Arty with us out of pure love and affection, so that the darling should never be cuffed about, or reminded or taunted with his heart-broken parents' crime'.

That night in the summer of 1887, Francis Thompson faced suicide alone with only his deadly doses of laudanum for company, but one effect of the opium in the tincture meant that, after he had taken the first dose, he soon acquired an unexpected companion. This was a young man he immediately recognised as the poet Thomas Chatterton, whose appearance at this time was a surprise, since Chatterton had actually killed himself with arsenic in London in 1770, nearly one hundred and twenty years earlier.

Chatterton's ghost advised Thompson not to take his second, fatal dose because he, Chatterton, had by bad luck killed himself the day before an enthusiastic fan called Doctor Thomas Fry had arrived in London, intending to rescue him from his poverty. Assuring Thompson that there was someone very like his Dr Fry just around his personal corner, Chatterton managed to persuade Francis Thompson to abandon his suicide attempt then and there.

If nothing else, the fact that Thomas Chatterton popped into Thompson's brain while it was nearly drowning in opium suggests that Francis was on some level at least thinking about being a poet, even though he had not made much impression as a poet up to that time. The Chatterton vision also confirms that Thompson had an awareness of the heritage of English poetry: in later years, he would write essays about earlier poets and poetry that would illuminate his own poetic thought-processes.

There are accounts of many people as desperate as Thompson was in the days before his attempted suicide in Booth's *Darkest England*. Many of them are living on the streets of London – starving and unable even to afford a bed for the night in one of the notorious, cheap doss-houses of the Victorian capital, simply because they are unemployed. Some are trapped in a deadly downward spiral: at first they cannot find work, and so they starve, and life on the streets makes their appearance disreputable, so possible employers reject them. Starvation soon weakens them, and they are unable to work well even when they find employment. Booth explains that the workhouses designed to deal with this social problem offer little help: to 'pay' for the pitiful food and lodgings the paupers find there, they are forced to stay inside the workhouse for a set amount of time, so that they are unable to look for work outside. Meanwhile, inside the workhouse, they are forced to do such typical convicts' work as breaking stones or picking oakum, which further saps their strength. Arthur, the chemist who made the failed family suicide pact, stated in a letter that he would rather die than enter a workhouse.

It is hardly surprising that the denizens of the streets whom Booth's salvationists encountered should have turned to laudanum or alcohol to relieve their misery, and the General is sympathetic about some whose descent into actual crime he chronicles. He admits, however, that some of London's poor are naturally idle and actually unwilling to work, even though work might save their lives; and some have coarse, stubborn characters that make them unsuitable for any type of employment.

By no means all the tough cases immortalised in *Darkest England* are unskilled or uneducated people, and some had evidently fallen from lives of considerable comfort because of old age or illness. Some are literate and experienced clerks who have benefited from a degree of education, but Booth laments that these men are merely qualified to join the long ranks of those competing for the small number of clerking jobs.

One result of such widespread and desperate unemployment, Booth asserts, is to make the employed people who work hard to maintain themselves in a station just above the jobless feel less secure. At any time, they could be replaced by desperate newcomers willing to work longer hours, in worse conditions, and for less pay.

One of the factors that anyone making a study of Jack the Ripper has to understand is the sheer misery of many people living in the Ripper's part of

London when the killer was still a threat. No less a person than the playwright George Bernard Shaw pointed out in a letter to the *Star* newspaper in September 1888 that the Whitechapel murderer had done a service to the poor of the East End by highlighting their plight. Jack, says Shaw, has even made the right-wing press more sympathetic, by converting them 'to an inept sort of Communism'. 'Private enterprise has succeeded where Socialism failed,' Shaw writes. 'Whilst we conventional Social Democrats were wasting our time on education, agitation, and organisation, some independent genius has taken the matter in hand.'

For many cases described in William Booth's book, they have no sources of help left, and no hope. Arthur, the suicidal chemist of Holloway, wrote that just three pounds sent from an unnamed wealthy uncle, who would regard such a sum as a mere 'flea-bite', would have saved his family. This amount in 1890 would be equivalent to about two hundred pounds today; but the miserly uncle would not send it. A strange fact relating to Francis Thompson's time down and out in London, which lasted for three years to the Ripper year of 1888, is that by contrast he had alternatives to destitution, periods of employment and also relatives in London and elsewhere on whom he could have called for help. And unlike many others who acquired their opium addiction and similar bad habits on the streets, Thompson was probably an opium addict before he arrived in London to make a life for himself there, in 1885.

2. Childhood of a Monster?

Born in the town of Preston in Lancashire in 1859, Francis Thompson was the first of three surviving children of Charles Thompson, a busy Catholic doctor: this was precisely the kind of background that would have given Thompson many advantages for the future, and could have given him an early boost into a secure, productive and successful life.

Charles Thompson was a homeopathic doctor – a type of physician described in Ambrose Bierce's *Devil's Dictionary* (1911) as 'the humorist of the medical profession'. From time to time, there are 'exposés' of this type of medicine, which is supposed to rely on the ancient principle that it is a good idea to treat an illness with a little of something that resembles the illness. Opponents of homeopathy (which, incidentally, is a medical approach very much favoured by the current Queen of England) point out that the alleged active ingredients of homeopathic medicines are present in such infinitesimally small concentrations that they could not possibly have an effect on any patient. Today homeopathy is firmly categorised as a form of 'alternative' medicine, but the lines between 'quack' medicine and 'conventional' or scientific medicine were not so strictly drawn in Victorian times, when medical knowledge was still in an extremely primitive state. Another Jack the Ripper suspect called Francis: the American 'Doctor' Francis Tumblety, was described as an 'Indian herb doctor', yet (at least according to his own publicity) he was widely respected as a useful physician.

Unlike many Victorian families, the Thompsons had a number of children that was quite close to the modern British average, although tragically this happened partly because Francis's older brother died at birth in the year before Francis was born. The family finances were not, therefore, stretched by the challenge of providing for swarms of children. As the only surviving son, Francis was the only one the family had to support through school and college, in those days when the education of girls was widely considered to be far less important than that of boys.

The poet's birthplace links him with another popular Jack the Ripper suspect, who was also born in Preston. This was James Kelly, born just a few months after Thompson. Because of his later links to the United States, Kelly features in my book *American Jack* (2017). This particular Preston-born Ripper suspect was condemned to death after stabbing his wife in the neck, right in front of her mother, in the summer of 1883. When it became clear that he was quite insane, Kelly's death sentence was commuted to life imprisonment at Broadmoor Psychiatric Hospital in Berkshire. Kelly managed to escape, and stayed at large in Europe and America for many years. It was during his years on the run that James is thought by some to have committed the Ripper murders.

In 1864 the Thompsons moved from Preston to the Manchester suburb of Ashton-under-Lyne, where they were unfortunate enough to be present during a serious anti-Catholic riot in 1868. As if the Thompsons did not already know that adhering to the Roman Catholic religion made them outsiders in the eyes of some of their contemporaries, the events in Ashton in the May of 1868 showed that some Englishmen were still so fanatically anti-Catholic that they were prepared to engage in dangerous pitched battles – where revolvers were used – to show their disdain for 'the old religion'.

Ironically, the Ashton riot and many others were stirred up not by an Englishman but by an Irishman, from Limerick, who had been baptised a Catholic, but converted to Protestantism. This was the odious William Murphy, who specialised in inflammatory, rabble-rousing speeches on the supposed corruption and unrestrained vice to be found among the Catholic clergy. 'I am for war with the knife, war with revolver if you like, war with the bayonet if you like,' Murphy used to say, and he and an assistant would act out the method by which they claimed confessionals were used as places of assignation by Catholic priests. According to Murphy, there was a kind of white slave trade of girls and women who were kidnapped by Catholics and forced to serve the holy fathers in secret harems.

By a miracle, only one person is known to have died during the Ashton riots, a lady called Mary Bradby. At first it was thought that she had been trampled to death, but then it emerged that she had had a serious heart condition, and had probably died of fright. Over a hundred Catholic houses were broken into and trashed, as were some local Catholic chapels. Reflecting on the riots, a journalist on W.T. Stead's paper the *Pall Mall Gazette* showed an astounding lack of enlightenment by stating that 'Such an insignificant creature as Murphy' was able to light 'such a fire as this' because 'the overwhelming majority of Englishmen of all ranks of life do from their very hearts, and in a great variety of ways, utterly detest superstition and priestcraft.' 'Superstition and priestcraft' were supposed to be characteristics of Roman Catholicism.

Stead's *Pall Mall Gazette* would later cover the Ripper murders with some relish: Stead himself also helped General William Booth in the task of writing the aforementioned book *In Darkest England*.

It has been argued that Francis Thompson's awareness of the Ashton riot (he would have been nine years old at the time) might have twisted his impressionable young mind in some way, and begun the psychological changes that led to his becoming Jack the Ripper. This seems a bit of a stretch, as no murders are known to have been deliberately committed at this time, and even if some of the combatants had fallen in the heat of battle, they would probably not have been eviscerated at the scene, as some of the Ripper's victims were. For a man to shoot, stab or beat another man to death in the heat of a riot is quite different from cold-bloodedly hunting down a woman in a dark, deserted street and ripping up her abdomen.

With a child's keen hearing, Thompson might have heard some of the disturbing sounds of the riot, so much like the sounds of a regular battle, from the safety of the family home. It may be that this experience fed into the poet's later fascination with war and battles.

It is unlikely that any of the Thompsons took part in the Ashton riot, though the fact that such violence could be inspired by the religion about which they were very serious may have reinforced the family's feeling of social isolation. As Brigid Boardman points out in *From Heaven to Charing Cross*, her 1988 biography of Francis Thompson, English Catholics like the Thompsons could find themselves considered outsiders not just by English Protestants, but also by Catholics from Ireland such as the ones that had fought the Protestants on the streets of Ashton. The Thompsons were also different, in terms of background and religious attitudes, from the old English Catholic families, many of them based in the north, who had not become Protestant at the Reformation, and had stayed loyal to Catholicism for centuries.

Charles and Mary, Francis Thompson's parents, were both from families that had turned to Catholicism in relatively recent years, and they were enthusiastic enough about their Church to be willing to encourage their only son to aim at the priesthood. They also encouraged a daughter (Francis's sister Mary) to become a nun. If these two children had both taken up their religious vocations, then their parents' chances of ever having grandchildren would have relied on the remaining daughter, Margaret. As it happens, Mary did become a nun, Francis did not become a priest, but it was still left to Margaret to produce the next generation.

At the age of ten, Francis was sent over a hundred miles north from Ashton to boarding-school at a Catholic college in County Durham. This was St Cuthbert's College at Ushaw, just a few miles west of Durham City. Since Francis himself is supposed to have wanted to become a priest at this time, Ushaw must have seemed to his parents to be a good place to start. There boys could experience a Catholic boarding school education, and, if they were found to have a genuine vocation for the priesthood, could continue on the same campus and enter the Ushaw seminary.

Today, visitors to the Ushaw complex are often surprised by the sheer size of the place, which of course had to be big enough to incorporate, among other things, schools, a college, libraries, dormitories, refectories, chapels, offices and sports-fields. Founded in 1808, the college was a successor to the English Catholic college at Douai in France, which itself had been founded in the sixteenth century so that Catholic Englishmen could train to be priests at a time when adherents of their religion were being cruelly persecuted in England.

In its early days, the Douai College sent newly-trained priests back to England to sustain and promote their religion in the face of official government resistance. Many of these men were hanged, drawn and quartered as traitors in Elizabethan times, and it is likely that as a schoolboy at Ushaw Thompson would have learned about these grisly martyrdoms, some of which took place in or near the city of Durham.

Hanging, drawing and quartering involves an

element of Ripper-style evisceration: the victim's heart is supposed to be pulled out while he is still alive, and his intestines thrown into boiling water, along with his genitals. The passing on of stories of these and other martyrdoms was once regarded as an essential part of Christian education: martyrdom was regarded as a glorious and inspiring thing. The *Acts and Monuments* of John Foxe, an Elizabethan convert to Protestantism from Catholicism, was a massive best-seller for many decades, and the standard reference book of saints was written by the eighteenth-century English Catholic priest Alban Butler. Foxe's book is also known as *Foxe's Book of Martyrs*.

Some of the imagery found in Thompson's poetry evokes wounds, blood, pain and death, and is explicitly drawn from central Christian stories such as the crucifixion of Jesus. Could it be that the mayhem at Ashton in 1868, combined with Christian tales of torture and death, turned an innocent Catholic schoolboy into a serial killer?

At Ushaw, the boys were routinely beaten as part of the disciplinary regime – something that was regarded as quite normal at the time. 'Caning' and other types of corporal punishment were widely used in English schools until very recently; but even though Francis is known to have been beaten at school, the fact of his having been sent away to boarding-school at all might seem strange to readers unfamiliar with the attitudes to childhood and education still found among many middle- and upper-class people in England. Boys in particular are still routinely sent away to board at 'prep' schools from the age of eight, and the 'old boys' of these schools and the 'better' 'public' schools still dominate the upper echelons of politics, business and the arts. The deleterious psychological consequences of this type of abrupt childhood separation from the family home have been well-documented, and whole books could be filled with true tales of the abuse meted out to these unfortunate children. But still the custom persists, and many powerful people continue to argue that it really cannot be dispensed with.

The shock of suddenly finding himself away from home among boys of his own age must have been particularly acute for Thompson, as he had had no brothers at home, played at dolls and cricket with his sisters, and had not attended a primary school, having been educated at home. His anguish increased when the other boys started to single him out for physical and psychological torment: something they may have been driven to by their own sense of vulnerability in their new surroundings. His account of his sufferings at this time is unsettlingly vivid:

The malignity of my tormentors was more heart-lacerating than the pain itself. It seemed to me – virginal to the world's ferocity – a hideous thing that strangers should dislike me, should delight and triumph in pain to me, though I had done them no ill and bore them no malice; that malice should be without provocative malice. That seemed to me dreadful, and a veritable demoniac revelation. Fresh from my tender home, and my circle of just-judging friends, these malignant school-mates who danced round me with mocking evil distortion of laughter – God's good laughter, gift of all things that look back the sun – were to me devilish apparitions of a hate now first known; hate for hate's sake, cruelty for cruelty's sake. And as such they live in my memory, testimonies to the murky aboriginal demon in man.

That the adult Thompson continued to be haunted by these demonic boys, who seemed to be temporarily possessed by some abstract power of evil, may suggest that his mind had been alerted at this time to the dark forces that some say lurk in all human beings, including his previously unsuspecting self. Once recognised, these forces, which often surface in his poetry, could not be unrecognised, and some of the things he saw in later life may only have served to reinforce his sense of the shadows lurking in the corners of the mind. Had he gazed into the abyss, and had the abyss begun to speak to him?

Thompson's first, startled glimpse at pure evil resurfaced when he wrote an essay about the poet Shelley (1792-1822). Commenting on how Shelley also suffered torment at the hands of his schoolmates, he gave an insight into how deeply he felt his own sense of isolation and rejection at this time. Here he is trying to recapture the sense of utter, all-consuming grief that children can experience simply because they do not have the emotional checks and balances that adults generally have. This will be evident to anyone who has seen a child completely overcome by grief or pain, something that can be prompted by the silliest little thing:

Children's griefs are little, certainly; but so is the child, so is its endurance, so is its field of vision, while its nervous impressionability is keener than ours. Grief is a matter of relativity: the sorrow should be estimated by its proportion to the sorrower: a gash is as painful to one as an amputation to another. Pour a puddle into a thimble, or an Atlantic into Etna; both thimble and mountain overflow.

Thompson's essay on Shelley, regarded as one of his better prose pieces, shows him once again turning to another poet to make sense of his own life, as his opium-deluded brain did when he was on the verge of suicide in 1887, and thought he saw the shade of Thomas Chatterton. In the Shelley essay, Thompson identifies so closely with Shelley that some would say he misjudges the man, making the author of *Ozymandias* too much like himself:

So beset, the child [Shelley] fled into the tower of his own soul, and raised the drawbridge. He threw out a reserve, encysted in which he grew to maturity unaffected by the intercourses that modify the maturity of others into the thing we call a man.

This is probably a fair description of Thompson as a child, literally hiding behind his books and fantasies, but Shelley was of an altogether different temperament. Shelley turned his feelings about the torment he suffered as a child into a life of rebellion, of 'kicking against the pricks', determined to stand out against every manifestation of authority and convention. Shelley did not 'opt out' as Thompson did: he was so engaged in rebellion that he was ejected from university, closely watched by the government, and cut off by his family.

Or can it be that, inside his inner castle and behind his drawbridge, Thompson's grief was turning into anger, ready to be released in a prolonged murder-spree that offended every possible standard of human decency?

Thompson's birthplace

Portrait by Everard Meynell

> Bishop's House
> Pantasaph
> Wednesday.
>
> Dearest Wilfrid & Alice,
>
> &c you are together in my thoughts, so let me join you together in this note. I cannot express to you what deep happiness your visit gave me; how dear it was to see your faces again. I think "the leaves fell from the day," indeed, when your train went out of the station; and I never heard the birds with such bad voices.

Sample of Thompson's handwriting

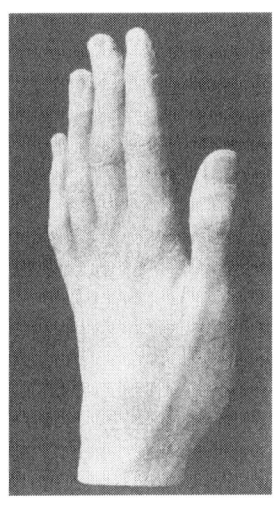

Cast of Thompson's hand

Ushaw College

Life-mask

In later life

3. The Outcast

According to the biography published by his younger friend Everard Meynell in 1913, Thompson's contemporaries at Ushaw, both teachers and boys, did not remember him as being deeply troubled; but Meynell's book does convey an impression of an odd, eccentric school-boy, given to the solitary occupation of reading, not much enamoured with sports, feeble though upright in body, with a strong tendency to get the top prize in English composition. In 1872 Father Nowlan, a priest at Ushaw who was also a friend of the Thompson family, wrote to Ashton saying that Francis's last set of examinations had yielded results that were:

. . . very satisfactory indeed – second in Latin and first in English, his master was speaking to me about him yesterday, and said that his English composition was the best production from a lad of his age which he had ever seen in this seminary.

This was no more than was to be expected for a future poet, but the good Father went on to mention a fault in Francis that he hoped would now fall away: a certain absent-mindedness that had been 'a great obstacle to his application to study'.

In his biography of the poet, Everard Meynell gives an affectionate account of how Thompson's absent-mindedness stayed with him, and perhaps increased, in adulthood. It seems that he was the last person on earth to turn up on time for anything, and Meynell suggests that at times he was quite unaware of the time of day:

His was a long series of broken trysts – trysts with the sunrise, trysts with Sunday mass, obligatory but impossible; trysts with friends. Whether it was indolence or, as he explained it, an insurmountable series of detaining accidents, it is certain that he, captain of his soul, was not captain of his hours. They played him false at every stroke of the clock, mutinied with such cunning that he would keep an appointment in all good faith six hours after it was past. Dismayed, he would emerge from his room upon a household preparing for dinner, when he had lain listening to sounds he thought betokened breakfast.

One distraction from the books he was supposed to study at Ushaw were any poetry books Thompson could get his hands on, although he was known as a skilled writer of prose, and not poetry, at school. He would sit for hours reading and copying poems, hiding behind a wall of books erected to conceal this mildly illicit activity.

Father Nowlan's optimistic feeling that Francis's absent-mindedness would soon wear off is contradicted by another letter sent from the school to the Thompson home, in June 1877. The President of the College himself wrote to Thompson's father that despite his docility, obedience and cleverness, Frank's 'strong, nervous timidity' meant that the President and other members of the College staff were forced to conclude 'that it is not the holy will of God that he should go on for the Priesthood'. Suggesting that it was now high time he set his mind to another future profession, the President also mentioned what, in the long run, may have been a far more serious fault in 'Frank' than his timidity: 'a natural indolence which has always been an obstacle with him', which he needed to shake off.

It may be that the Thompsons' only son had been caught in one of the paradoxes of school life: the qualities required to do well at school are not necessarily the same as those needed to succeed in a future career. The young Thompson was docile and bookish, qualities which endeared him to his teachers, who probably dreaded hyper-active boys with no taste for reading; but those very extrovert, sleeves-rolled-up boys probably made the best professionals when school was left behind.

The Thompson family did not look far to find a second career path for Francis. He was sent to Owens College in Manchester to train as a doctor, which was of course his father's profession. This was an extreme case of a phenomenon that can still be seen today in universities all over the world: the student who is following the course his parents want him to follow, which is however of no interest to him, his real interests and talents lying somewhere else. Francis Thompson was not only not interested in medicine: he seems to have loathed everything about it, and tried to engage with his course as little as possible, visiting art galleries and libraries, in the latter of which he read widely quite outside the field of medicine. Then as now, aspiring doctors were required to dissect human bodies, something that a 'sensitive' boy like 'Frank' could not take to. The grisly sights he saw lying on cold slabs at that time stayed with him and resurfaced in his later poetry. But did he try to re-enact those dissections with living subjects on the streets of London in 1888?

It is likely that Thompson's father knew perfectly well that 'Frank' would flunk his medical training, or, if he managed by some miracle to scrape a pass in his final exams, would make a very poor physician. Indolence (which is a polite word for 'laziness') and absent-mindedness are not qualities that are compatible with the medical profession, and it is likely that Thompson was also physically clumsy and uncoordinated, so that even simple procedures such as lancing boils may have been quite beyond him.

It is not clear exactly when or why Thompson became addicted to laudanum, but if he was in thrall to the drug when he was in effect pretending to be a medical student, then that would have made him even less convincing as a trainee medic. It may be he started taking laudanum to distract him from the horrors of the hospital and the dissecting-room, or just as a cheap alternative to alcohol. He might have attended a lecture on opium's amazing properties, and decided to try it out for himself, or, more likely, it was prescribed for him by a local doctor in Manchester as a cure for some physical ailment.

Laudanum can suppress a cough and also act as

an effective counter-measure against diarrhoea. Since Frank could easily have caught colds and coughs, and since cholera and dysentery were frequent visitors to the streets of Victorian England, the future poet may have been prescribed laudanum to help with the symptoms of those diseases. Laudanum was often prescribed to help with the symptoms of tuberculosis at the time, but in her 1988 biography of the poet, Brigid Boardman offers proof that Thompson may never have suffered from tuberculosis, though it was tragically prevalent, even endemic, in parts of Victorian society.

Today we have medicines that act specifically on symptoms such as coughs and diarrhoea, but laudanum was commonly self-prescribed, or prescribed by medics, for those symptoms in those days. In modern terms, this is a little like buying a huge aeroplane simply because one wants to visit a city two miles away – laudanum supplied far more than it was asked for in cases of severe coughing or diarrhoea.

If opium in one form or another was not actually prescribed or recommended for Thompson, then it may have been the experience of watching his dying mother draw comfort from the drug that led him to it. Mary Thompson died of a liver problem in the December of 1880, and, significantly, her last present to her son was Thomas de Quincey's autobiographical book *Confessions of an English Opium Eater,* a classic account of addiction.

In all, Thompson spent six years not-quite training as a doctor, failing end-of-year exams (that could not be taken in Manchester, but had to be sat in Edinburgh or London), re-taking parts of the course and generally wasting everybody's time, and his family's money. The course should have lasted only four years, and at last, probably in 1884, it was clear that medicine was not, and could never be, for him.

He attempted to start again, in a profession related to that of a doctor – the manufacture of surgical instruments; but he also failed in that. He was then taken on as a salesman of encyclopaedias, but did nothing but read the entire set of encyclopaedias. He spent a short time in the army, but was thrown out because of his poor health. At last, in November 1885, he decided to leave the family home at Ashton and look for a new way of life in London. His father had questioned his son about his odd behaviour and flushed appearance: was he drinking too much alcohol? Thompson answered, quite truthfully, that he was not. It is likely that his widowed father's plan to re-marry merely added to Thompson's feeling that he could no longer find a home at home.

At first, Thompson found employment in London carrying a sack of books from a wholesaler between various book-shops in the capital. No doubt because of his laziness, absent-mindedness and bookishness (which may have tempted him to read the books rather than delivering them) this job went the way of the instrument-making job and the job as a salesman of encyclopaedias.

Everard Meynell's biography of his older friend paints a disconcerting picture of how Thompson's abstraction and absent-mindedness increased exponentially when he was a seemingly hopeless, unemployed, drug-addled outcast in London. Time ceased to have any meaning at all, and he often did not know whether minutes or hours had passed between one incident, or sight seen, and another. As well as time, space seemed to become horribly variable: 'Oxford Street was short and narrow; Wardour Street big enough to hold the tribes of Israel, and the houses of it as high, he guessed, thought he dared not lift his head to see, as the divided waves of the Red Sea'.

There was also some sort of bizarre interference tinkering with his senses, so that sometimes he seemed to be watching a silent film, while at other times sounds only came to him some time after everyone else had heard them.

Unemployed, Thompson kept his head above water for a while by remembering to collect the seven shillings a week, worth perhaps twenty pounds today, that his father sent him. No doubt Charles Thompson could have afforded more, but if he thought his son was an alcoholic, or suspected that he was a laudanum addict, he may have restricted the amount, hoping that 'Frank' would spend it first on essentials, and have none left for intoxicants. By now, however, laudanum may have become more important to Francis than food and lodgings. But soon even his allowance was neglected, the money was stopped because it was not being claimed, and Francis slid slowly into abject poverty, homelessness and life on the streets.

Although he had certainly brought this fate upon himself, it may be that some bitterness against people he blamed at this time comes out in his later poetry. Annie Richardson, who was soon to become his step-mother, may be the 'wicked', 'evil' and actually cannibalistic step-mother of his *Ballad of Fair Weather*; and Nature herself becomes a cruel step-mother in Thompson's most celebrated poem, *The Hound of Heaven*:

Nature, poor stepdame, cannot slake my drouth;
Let her, if she would owe me,
Drop yon blue bosom-veil of sky, and show me
The breasts o' her tenderness:
Never did any milk of hers once bless
My thirsting mouth.

Can it be that Thompson's bitterness, perhaps directed at his step-mother in these poems, expressed itself not just in poetry, but in physical violence against women who were for the most part somewhat older than he was, in the Ripper year of 1888, the year after his father's second marriage?

Whether or not he later became Jack the Ripper, Thompson went through a long period serving as a victim of Victorian society's ability to ignore the terrible conditions it reserved for the workless poor. Francis came to know the capital's low doss-houses, and the cold charity of the work-houses described by William Booth. When he could not earn enough money by holding people's horses, opening cab doors, carrying parcels, selling matches and the like, the future poet slept on the streets. In his *Sister Songs* he writes about how:

Once—in that nightmare-time which still doth haunt
My dreams, a grim, unbidden visitant—
Forlorn, and faint, and stark,
I had endured through watches of the dark
The abashless inquisition of each star,
Yea, was the outcast mark
Of all those heavenly passers' scrutiny;
Stood bound and helplessly
For Time to shoot his barbed minutes at me;
Suffered the trampling hoof of every hour
In night's slow-wheeled car;
Until the tardy dawn dragged me at length
From under those dread wheels; and, bled of strength
I waited the inevitable last.

By any standard, this is a powerful depiction of the 'nightmare-time' Thompson endured, and the lines printed above may even record some of the hallucinatory effects of opium on the future poet's perceptions. As he sleeps out under the stars (not as romantic as it sounds when you are starving on a London street) the stars seem to be interrogating him, staging their own 'inquisition': a reference, perhaps, to one of the most notorious aspects of Catholic history. The stars subject him to 'scrutiny'; they have become like living beings, like the inanimate objects that became animals in de Quincey's opium dreams. Time itself is personified here, and seems to be shooting its 'barbed minutes' like arrows at Thompson. Night itself has or becomes a 'car' or chariot, and the horses drawing night on trample the poor rough-sleeper.

When he was not trying desperately to scrape enough money together to buy a bed for the night, something to eat and some laudanum (not necessarily in that order) Thompson would seek warmth and shelter in the Guildhall Library, until his appearance deteriorated to the point where he was refused admittance. He also spent time in the National Gallery, where his innocent attempt to inform an ignorant lady about the subject of a painting made him realise how far he had fallen below the level of the comfortable middle classes who could discuss such things with strangers of similar status. Of course the lady would not discuss art with a scruffy tramp. Scorned and rejected by strangers, the recipient of cold charity, abandoned to 'the inevitable last', did rage begin to stir, or stir again, in Francis Thompson?

4. The Land of the Bare Shank-Bone

After the loss of both his allowance from home and his job carting books around, Francis Thompson was indeed in dire straits; but a complete stranger did go out of his way to help. This was John McMaster, owner of a boot shop in Panton Street, just off Leicester Square, who was also deeply involved in the life of the Anglican church of St Martin-in-the-Fields, on nearby Trafalgar Square.

St Martin's has not, of course, been 'in the fields' for a long time: it now stands in the heart of what is perhaps the busiest part of Westminster, a portion of London that was once separated from the more easterly City of London by a stretch of open country. The present church, which was re-built in the eighteenth century, does not look like the typical English medieval church with Gothic arches; a model that was endlessly re-hashed by the architects of Francis Thompson's own century. St Martin's is classical in design, and could be mistaken for a Greek temple, a fine customs-house or even the headquarters of a long-established bank.

St Martin's has been active in charity work for many years, and in Thompson's time its trustees administered almshouses for women. Today the church does very useful work with London's homeless, especially the younger modern rough-sleepers who still live as Francis Thompson did during the grim nadir of his life. Figures for 2015 estimate that there were over seven and a half thousand such people in London at that time, equivalent to the population of a town like Launceston in Cornwall, or Greenville, Rhode Island in the United States.

Through a charity called The Connection at St Martin-in-the-Fields, the church helps the homeless, for instance through a programme of 'street outreach', which involves volunteers going out at all hours every day, offering help and advice to homeless people.

'Street outreach' would be a good name for what John McMaster tried with Francis Thompson, though McMaster was using his own initiative and resources and seems not to have relied on any larger organisation for help or advice. He simply saw the by now pale, gaunt and shabby figure of Francis Thompson trying to sell matches in the street, and asked him, 'Is your soul saved?'

Thompson seems to have surprised McMaster by replying with another question, 'What right have you to ask that question?' Apparently unfazed, McMaster offered, 'If you won't let me save your soul, let me save your body.'

What McMaster was offering was something he had already offered to a number of young men who had benefited enormously from his help. This was the opportunity to do paid work at McMaster's boot shop in Panton Street, to live in a lodging that

McMaster would set up for him, and to learn the skills of repairing, making and selling boots, as well as the other skills required in a combined workshop and retail outlet. These included running errands, taking off the shutters at the start of the day, and putting them back up again at night. His food, lodgings, a medical check-up and some new clothes were all paid for by McMaster, and Francis received an additional five shillings a week.

Perhaps inevitably, Thompson proved to be completely useless as an apprentice in a boot shop: he spent a lot of time writing in disused account-books, dreaming, chatting to customers and exhibiting his clumsy abstraction by, for instance, hurting the foot of a customer by dropping a shutter on it. He could also be tetchy and restless, prone to shout alarmingly if crossed in an argument.

In the end, McMaster was forced to sack Thompson, who in later years he recalled as his only failure. Like Thompson's father, the boot-maker assumed that it was alcohol that was causing Thompson's erratic behaviour.

Apart from new clothes, shelter, medical attention and regular meals over the six short months that the arrangement limped along, one lasting benefit came out of McMaster's attempt to save Francis: the latter started to write again in earnest, and attempted to put some things together in prose, while his crucifix loomed above him in his Southampton Row lodgings.

In his biography of the poet, Everard Meynell was able to supply plenty of detail about McMaster's attempt to save Francis Thompson, because he, Meynell, was able to track down McMaster himself and interview him. Much less is known about the second person who made a serious attempt to save Francis – an unnamed prostitute who took Thompson in and allowed him to eat and sleep with her in her room in Chelsea. After the third, successful attempt to save Thompson started to work, Thompson himself tried to track down this street girl 'with a heart of gold', but he could not find her, so it was unlikely that Thompson's biographer could ever have found her years later.

This might be a good place to remind readers that London's demographic was quite different in the late nineteenth century from what it is now, in the early twenty-first. Chelsea is now a very expensive place to live, and has become a by-word for a certain kind of rich, entitled person. It was certainly not so when it served as a bolt-hole for Francis Thompson and his mysterious street-girl. Likewise, the Meynells, who later rescued Thompson from his life on the streets, were not millionaires, although they lived in Kensington.

It seems that both Thompson and the street-girl were out and about during the day, she at her work and he drifting around more or less aimlessly as usual – she would pick him up in a hired horse-drawn cab on the way home, and they would share their evenings and nights together. Thompson seems to have taken up with this girl after his attempted suicide in the summer of 1887.

Whether sleeping with this girl, or perhaps in the same room, means that their relationship became sexual is unclear. As presented by Everard Meynell, and in symbolic form in some of Thompson's later poetry, the whole thing is shrouded in mystery and ambiguity; but it is likely that after servicing customers all day, sex would have been the last thing on the girl's mind. It may be that she acted as a kind of mother to Francis, or that he was able to recapture with her some of the spirit of his relationship with his sisters when they were all children together. If he was still taking sufficiently large doses of laudanum, which like many opiates suppresses the libido, then Thompson also may have been quite uninterested in sex. Add to that his general ill-health, which persisted even when he was clear of opium, his Catholic background, his *de facto* training for the celibate Roman Catholic priesthood, and the sexual repressiveness of Victorian middle-class culture, and we can begin to see how this pair may have avoided anything really sexual.

Readers familiar with the life of the aforementioned Thomas de Quincey will notice some striking similarities between Thompson's experiences in London and those of the author of the *Confessions of an Opium Eater*. Both lived on the streets, both deliberately avoided chances to save themselves, both were addicted to opium (though de Quincey generally ate his, and did not always drink it in the form of laudanum), both were obsessed with poets and poetry, both went on to become fine essayists, and both were befriended by prostitutes when they were down and out in London. And de Quincy insists in his *Confessions* that he did not have sex with 'his' prostitute, not least because his addiction had caused all his interest in the opposite sex to be suppressed.

Given these remarkable similarities, some have suggested that Thompson, who had of course been given de Quincey's *Confessions* as a present from his dying mother, and who later wrote a fine assessment of the earlier writer's work, may have invented some incidents in his life on the streets so as to emulate de Quincey. Certainly he copied him in the matter of always having two books in his pockets: one of English poetry and one of ancient Greek plays.

It is also possible that at some point Thompson became determined to experience what de Quincey had experienced in London, which might explain why he seems to have deliberately frustrated McMaster's determined attempt to save him. This might also explain why he never asked for help from those of his relations who lived in London: his paternal grandmother lived in the City Road, an uncle lived in Hinde Street, Manchester Square, and some other relatives ran a stationery shop on the Strand.

De Quincey lost Ann, 'his' prostitute, who it seems was only fifteen, and despite desperate attempts to find her, he never recovered her again. That Thompson also failed to find 'his' prostitute suggests that in her case she made a deliberate effort to get away from him and become unfindable. He knew where she lodged in Chelsea, and he knew where she generally solicited customers – in the Strand, a long street that connects Charing Cross in the west to Fleet Street, running roughly parallel to the north bank of the Thames.

Everard Meynell suggests that her flight was this lady's last, best gift to Thompson: she left him because he had been saved, was acquiring a reputation as a writer, and would have found it very difficult, in those starchy days, to explain his friendship with a girl of the streets. But there is very little direct information about this, and it is possible that Thompson's erratic behaviour, which, as we have seen, could lead to angry shouting, turned to violence against this girl, and that she fled for her own protection.

If this is what happened, then Thompson's long, obsessional searches through London for the girl take on a rather more sinister air; and the way he presented her in his poetry was sheer hypocrisy. In the lines that follow directly on from those from *Sister Songs* which are quoted in the last chapter, Thompson wrote:

Then there came past
A child; like thee, a spring-flower; but a flower
Fallen from the budded coronal of Spring,
And through the city-streets blown withering.
She passed,—O brave, sad, lovingest, tender thing!
And of her own scant pittance did she give,
That I might eat and live:
Then fled, a swift and trackless fugitive.

This makes the unnamed girl or woman into an angelic, mystical creature, which is convenient for Everard Meynell's biography, which some see as part of a campaign to clean up the image of the poet.

In his more probing 1968 biography *Strange Harp, Strange Symphony* John Walsh draws the reader's attention to an unpublished poem of Thompson's, written around this time, where, Walsh suggests, Thompson's street-girl is presented in symbolic form as the deceptive temptress who lures 'a lusty night' into the nightmare landscape of the 'Land of the Bare Shank-Bone'. Here are two stanzas from this disturbing poem, the *Nightmare of the Witch-Babies*:

What is it sees he?
Ha! Ha!
There in the frightfulness?
Ho! Ho!
There he saw a maiden
Fairest fair:
Sad were her dusk eyes,
Long was her hair;
Sad were her dreaming eyes,
Misty her hair,
And strange was her garments' flow,
Two witch-babies, ho! ho! ho!

Swiftly he followed her,
Ha! Ha!
Eagerly followed her,
Ho! Ho!
From the rank, the greasy soil,
Red bubbles oozed and stood;
Till it grew a putrid slime,

And where'er his horse has trod,
The ground plash, plashes,
With a wet too like to blood;
And chill terrors like a fungus grow.
Two witch-babies, ho! ho! Ho!

In the next verse, the 'maiden fairest fair' reveals her true nature:

There stayed the maiden,
Ha! Ha!
Shed all her beauty;
Ho! Ho!
She shed her flower of beauty,
Grew laidly, old, and dire,
Was the demon-ridden witch,
And the consort of hell-fire:
'Am I lovely noble knight?
See thy hearts own desire!
Now they come, come upon thee, lo.
Two witch-babies, ho! ho! Ho!'

Next, the knight, who has been lured to this dreadful place by the maiden's deceptive looks, is attacked by the revolting 'witch babies' of the poem's title: personifications of Lust and 'Lust's disgust'.

The poem ends with advice to the reader to:

Shun the land, and shun the woman,
Shun the wicked spell

This can be read as Thompson's Victorian Catholic shame at his sexual relationship with a prostitute, but it can also be seen as a particularly nasty manifestation of misogyny, reminiscent of King Lear's tirade in Act 4 Scene 6 of Shakespeare's play:

Down from the waist they are centaurs, though women all above. But to the girdle do the gods inherit; beneath is all the fiends'. There's hell, there's darkness, there's the sulphurous pit— burning, scalding, stench, consumption! Fie, fie, fie, pah, pah!

If the *Witch Babies* poem really does reflect some deep-seated attitude of the poet, then it cannot be said that his attitude to women was altogether healthy or balanced. In the poem, the maiden starts off as beautiful, and she is identified as a maiden, meaning that she is a virgin, with sad eyes and 'misty' hair. She then turns abruptly into a 'demon-ridden witch'. In both manifestations, the maiden is symbolic rather than really human, which might suggest that at least at this period of his life, Thompson was having problems relating to women of about his own age as real people, sharing a common humanity. This may be why, when he was with McMaster, he developed such an attachment to the family's small daughter, with whom he could have a friendship without any hint of sexuality creeping in. Likewise, in his *Sister Songs*, he celebrates his friendship with female children, and laments the fact that they will eventually become women.

Any inability to see fellow-humans as humans, to see them only as potential threats or traps, or objects to be exploited, can be seen as a childish or adolescent trait; but it is also a characteristic of psychopaths.

5. Merry England

It seems that Francis Thompson's poem *The Nightmare of the Witch-Babies* was included in a packet of longhand manuscripts hand-posted by the poet through the letter-box of a magazine called *Merry England* in February 1887. The packet also contained other poems, and an essay called *Paganism Old and New*. The manuscript of the essay in particular was in a sorry state, a fact for which Thompson apologised in his covering letter:

In enclosing the accompanying article for your inspection I must ask pardon for the soiled state of the manuscript. It is due, not to slovenliness, but to the strange places and circumstances under which it has been written.

Though it may have been written in part in his room in Southampton Row, the poet had probably been carrying it around in his pocket ever since.

If any writer ever sent anything to a magazine in a half-hearted way, it was Thompson in February 1887. Francis ends his accompanying letter with the words, 'Kindly address your rejection to the Charing Cross Post Office', and in the body of the letter he says that he has included 'a few specimens' of his writing, on 'the off chance that one may be less poor than the rest'. Worse, he implies that if *Merry England* rejects him as a writer, he will not try anywhere else: 'I do not desire the return of the manuscript, regarding your judgement of its worthlessness as quite final'.

Merry England was a middle-brow magazine with a Roman Catholic slant, designed in part to give its readers an insight into cultural and social matters which, it was feared, many Catholics in Britain did not know enough about. The parents of the magazine were its editor Wilfrid Meynell, a convert to Catholicism who had been raised in the Quaker tradition, and his delicately beautiful wife Alice, also a convert, who was a noted poet in her own right.

It is unclear how long it took for Wilfrid to have a proper look at what Thompson had sent, but it was certainly long enough for Francis himself to give up hope. Just as he had stopped collecting his allowance from home, so he now stopped checking the Charing Cross Post Office for any messages, so the encouraging letters of acceptance that Meynell sent were not picked up. Unable to contact the writer by any other means, Meynell published Thompson's poem *The Passion of Mary* in the April 1888 edition of *Merry England*, hoping that it would attract the author's attention and encourage him to get in touch.

The April edition reached its subscribers in March, and Father John Carroll, a subscriber and an old Ashton friend of the Thompsons, contacted

Francis in London, advising him to tidy himself up and visit the *Merry England* offices. Although Carroll had enclosed some money to help Francis make himself look respectable, when Meynell finally received Thompson at the magazine's offices in Essex Street, just off the Strand:

a waif of a man came in. No such figure had been looked for; more ragged and unkempt than the average beggar, with no shirt beneath his coat and bare feet in broken shoes

From that moment, Thompson's future comfort and security were assured. As McMaster had done, the Meynells offered Thompson accommodation, hospitality, medical attention, an income, and regular work. The possible reasons why this rescue worked, in contrast to McMaster's effort, were that the Meynells offered Thompson work as a writer, not a boot-maker, and they also made him a part of their family and circle of friends. Here, in contrast to Paton Street, Francis could find sophisticated literary and religious conversation, and the company of kindred spirits.

What the Meynells and *Merry England* got in return was an important new writer of prose and, eventually, poetry, who was a committed Catholic in his own way, and could adjust his style to the agenda of *Merry England*. The new writer also had an interesting personal story, which must have increased his appeal for the magazine's readers. For Everard Meynell, one of the Meynells' six children, who was only six when the poet started coming to tea at Phillimore Street, the advent of Francis Thompson provided an interesting grown-up friend and the subject for the biography he published in 1913.

If the first doctor the Meynells set on Thompson was correct, it is likely that Francis would have died on the streets sometime in 1888 or 1889, if the poet's new friends had not intervened. Lovers of Thompson's writing must therefore feel grateful to the Meynells, though the use they made of their new protégé was not entirely blameless. As well as steering Thompson toward the kind of writing that would be acceptable to *Merry England* and other similar periodicals, the Meynells cleaned up his writings, editing out some disturbing elements, and persisted in presenting a squeaky-clean version of the poet's life. The following passage from Everard's biography is a good illustration:

The streets, somehow, had nurtured a poet and trained a journalist. He had gone down into poverty so absolute that he was often without pen and paper, and now emerged a pressman. Neither his happiness, nor his tenderness, nor his sensibility had been marred, like his constitution, by his experiences. To be the target of such pains as it is the habit of the world to deplore as the extreme of disaster, and yet to keep alive the young flame of his poetry; to be under compulsion to watch the ignominies of the town, and yet never to be nor to think himself ignominious; to establish the certitude of his virtue; to keep flourishing an infinite tenderness and capability for delicacies and *gentilezze* of love – these were the triumphs of his immunity.

Here Everard is painting a picture of a kind of male nineteenth-century Mother Teresa of Calcutta, who touched pitch, or got close to it, but was never defiled. The picture may arise not just from the Meynells' particular agenda, but also from the author's admiration for his lost friend, but it is still deeply unconvincing. The question that must be faced by anyone examining the possibility that Francis Thompson was Jack the Ripper is; did the Meynells unwittingly cover up something in the poet's past that was far worse than a suicide attempt, months of drug-taking, and a relationship with a prostitute?

This final, successful attempt to rescue Thompson did not happen all at once, and the timing and nature of the various stages in the change in Thompson's life at this time are unclear. Walsh tells us that Thompson had been set up in new lodgings, probably in Paddington, by the Meynells by December 1888, and that by then he was visiting their family home in Kensington almost every day. He had previously been sent by them to a private hospital to recover from his opium addiction, although a doctor had warned them that the writer's life was hanging by a thread and that the anguish of withdrawal might kill him.

Exactly when and where Thompson experienced 'cold turkey' in a hospital is unclear, and although it is likely that he was in lodgings by December 1888, it is not clear where he was living between the time the Meynells had started, in effect, to 'adopt' him as their protégé, and the last month of the year of the Ripper. It is also unclear at what stage his nameless street-girl left him and made herself unfindable. It may be that for a time the poet was sleeping rough again, or the Meynells may have given him money to secure beds in doss-houses; or perhaps, with Meynell money, Thompson was able to pay to stay in the street-girl's Chelsea lodgings on his own.

The business of what Francis Thompson was doing, where he was living, how sick or opium-addled he was, what his state of mind was and, particularly, what he looked like from the end of August to the beginning of November 1888 is important for what we might call his Jack the Ripper 'candidacy'.

Mary Ann Nichols, the first of the 'canonical' five Ripper victims, was found dead in Buck's Row (now Durward Street) in Whitechapel in the early morning of the last day of August 1888. The last victim, Mary Jane Kelly, was found just after 10:45 on the morning of the ninth of November 1888. There were two earlier murders that are sometimes attributed to the Ripper: those of Emma Smith in April 1888, and Martha Tabram on the seventh of August 1888. Francis Thompson was certainly in London over that period, but the circumstances of both murders, and the methods used, distinguish them from the canonical five.

The further we go through the end of 1888 and into the following years, the more difficult it becomes to imagine Thompson killing prostitutes on the streets of London. As his status, success and involvement with the Meynells grew, he spent more time out of the capital, for instance at Roman Catholic retreat houses. The original police files on the Ripper murders cover murders that occur as late as 1891, by which time Thompson was living a very different life to the one he had been living in London in 1888. Experts who believe that the Ripper murders finished with Mary Jane Kelly in November 1888 sometimes remark on the sudden cessation of the killings at that time: could it be that they stopped because the Meynells had unwittingly taken the Ripper off the streets?

In an endnote to his biography of Thompson, John Walsh remarks that part of the time Thompson is supposed to have spent searching for his lost street-girl coincided with the Ripper scare. Walsh remarks that Francis himself may have been questioned, but he does not suggest Thompson as a suspect. Joseph Rupp, a forensic pathologist from Texas, went further and suggested Thompson as a Ripper suspect in an article in the *Criminologist*, published to mark the centenary of the Ripper year, in 1988. Rupp's article is reprinted at the end of Richard Patterson's book *Jack the Ripper: The Works of Francis Thompson*.

Although nobody seems to have put Thompson in the frame for the Ripper murders before Rupp in 1988, the idea that the Ripper was a poet may date back as far as 1935, when R. Thurston Hopkins published his book *Life and Death at the Old Bailey.* Hopkins apologises for including a chapter on the Ripper, who had no connection to the Bailey, but explains that he learned many details of the case from an old officer there, who claimed to have been a policeman in the East End at the time, and to have witnessed the charnel-house the Ripper had made of Mary Jane Kelly's room.

Hopkins discusses a number of interesting Ripper suspects, then, near the end of his chapter, he reveals that he personally knew the Ripper. Hopkins' suspect, whom he gives the false name Mr Moring, was 'a poor devil-driven poet', a friend of both Mary Jane Kelly and Hopkins himself.

'Moring' and Hopkins would walk all over London together at night, talking. The poet had a long, dark face, lank, black hair and very scruffy clothes. He was a frequenter of opium dens who had been disowned by his parents, who ran a very respectable business in the East End. 'Moring', a very gentle man, would hold forth among his companions in all-night drinking-dens about the virtues of opium and the drawbacks of alcohol. Hopkins himself was first alerted to the possibility that his friend was the Ripper by the witness statement of one George Hutchinson, who claimed to have seen a man with Mary Jane Kelly shortly before she was killed.

Unfortunately, there is a great deal in Hutchinson's eye-witness account that does not match Hopkins' description of his friend 'Moring'. Although both men had black hair and dark complexions, and were of roughly the same height, Hutchinson's man looked too well-off to be a 'poor devil-driven poet'. Hopkins does not include Hutchinson's description of the man's turned-up moustache, heavy gold watch-chain or kid gloves, all of which indicated to Hutchinson that the man he had seen with Kelly was unusually well-off for someone who was visiting Whitechapel.

Hutchinson's description of the man he saw with

Kelly is so detailed, including the colour of the man's eye-lashes, that many experts have suspected him of making the man up, or elaborating on what he could remember of a man he had, after all, seen at night in a poorly-lit area, three whole days before he gave his witness-statement.

Whether he was a poet or not, and whether or not he was the man Hutchinson saw, there is little to link the man Hopkins claimed he knew with Francis Thompson. Both men were opium addicts, but 'Moring' frequented opium-dens and smoked opium, rather than drinking it in laudanum, though of course he may have done both. Thompson seems to have been too shy to have held forth to any drinking-companions, and his parents were a doctor and his wife at Ashton near Manchester, not local business people in the East End. Although it is possible that Thompson had a moustache at some point in 1888, I have yet to see any pictures of him that do not show him either clean-shaven or with a full beard. If Thompson never had a moustache without the rest of the set, even in 1888, then that set him apart from many adult male Londoners at the time, and many of the possible Ripper suspects seen by witnesses.

Yes, Thompson did walk around the streets of London at night; but then, many homeless people did: there was even a street-name for it: 'carrying the banner'.

The Moring-Thompson link is further tested by the possibility that 'Moring' was in fact another poet, Ernest Dowson (1867-1900).

Any attempt to link Thompson to the man

Hutchinson claimed he saw must contend with the fact that Hutchinson's man was clearly a snappy dresser with a good income. Even if the Meynells were funding him at this time, would Thompson have gone to the expense of buying a heavy gold watch-chain, spats and kid gloves? Such a get-up would have made Thompson look smart, in the British meaning of the word, even among the Meynells' well-off literary friends; but though his appearance did improve because of the application of *Merry England* money, he is still said to have looked shabby at the literary get-togethers in Kensington.

6. Possibilities

Even if the link to the man seen by George Hutchinson with Mary Jane Kelly, via Hopkins' 'poor devil-driven poet' seems tenuous, there is still good reason to include Francis Thompson on at least the long-list of Jack the Ripper suspects.

Thompson was a young man, living in London at the time of the murders, who is known to have associated with at least one prostitute – and all the canonical five victims were prostitutes. Thompson's youth counts in his favour as a suspect because sex killers (which is what Jack may have been) tend to be under forty.

Because of his resentment of his step-mother, Thompson may have had a grudge against women, particularly older women: it is sometimes forgotten that most of the canonical five victims were middle-aged, and probably looked older because of their drinking habits and the hardships they had endured, including malnutrition.

Thompson was on the streets of London for years, staying in various down-at-heel locations all over the city, so he might have known many useful short-cuts and bolt-holes that a murderer escaping from his prey could have used. This observation must, however, be tempered by Everard Meynell's assertion, in his 1913 biography of the poet, that Thompson regularly got lost in the streets, and was sometimes very surprised to find out where he actually was.

Disoriented or not, Thompson would no doubt also have known where prostitutes could be found, and when, and may even have known a number of the street-women by name. If they already knew him, his victims would have been more likely to trust him, even at the height of the Ripper scare. They may have been willing to go with him up dark alleys and into deserted squares. Although often aloof, abstracted and tongue-tied, Thompson could charm people, as he did his teachers at Ushaw and the boot-maker McMaster, and McMaster's colleagues and family. Was this just the well-documented superficial charm of the typical psychopath?

As a face regularly seen on the street, Francis may have gone unnoticed in certain districts. When he was at his dirtiest and scruffiest, people may have been fearful of catching his eye, as is often the case with derelict street-people. Scared to look at him for fear of becoming a target of his begging, verbal abuse or possibly insane conversation or behaviour, passers-by would not really see him, and would therefore not be able to remember him.

If, as is possible, Thompson had regular lodgings at this point, these would have been of great use to him if he actually was the Ripper, especially if they were in the overcrowded area of Whitechapel where most of the Ripper victims were found. Experts have long suspected that Jack, whoever he was, would have needed a safe, handy bolt-hole to flee to after his killings, where he could change, and perhaps wash any blood out of the clothes he had worn to perform the murders.

When (and if) Thompson found himself able to clean up his act after his first contact with the Meynells and *Merry England*, he may have appeared prosperous enough to lure prostitutes up dark alleys with believable offers of payment. He may not have been able to manage this when he was a derelict tramp.

Since the dawn of Ripperology, it has been suggested that the Ripper had some medical knowledge, and Thompson had had six years of medical training. He is also known to have possessed at least one scalpel in his life after Owens College; and he did work briefly for a medical instrument maker.

Much has been made of the fact that Thompson is supposed to have had a scalpel (presumably in some sort of case) to hand when he was on the London streets, but it was commonplace for men to have at least a pen-knife about them in those days, not so much for self-defence, but because such a thing has many uses. There is little evidence that a scalpel was used on Jack the Ripper's victims – pathologists at the time suggested that Jack's weapon of choice must have been a longer, stronger type of cutting instrument.

The Ripper was undoubtedly mad on some

level, and Thompson had been taking large doses of laudanum for years. Opium can induce symptoms similar to forms of madness such as schizophrenia, making it difficult for the patient to tell the difference between dreams, nightmare and reality. If he was trying to get off the drug during the year of the Ripper, withdrawal may have made Thompson restless and agitated. Violent and sexual feelings, which had been suppressed by the drug for so long, may have started to re-surface.

Since so little is known about the street-girl with whom Thompson spent time at Chelsea, all sorts of scenarios can be constructed around their relationship, many of which could give a novelist, for instance, a possible motive for the Ripper murders. Were Thompson and the girl lovers, and did she betray him in some way? Did she undergo an abortion to be rid of a child Thompson had fathered? Did this tip the Christian poet over the edge? Was he obsessively hunting for her in 1888, not to thank her and help her, but to confront her and 'punish' her?

Was he disgusted in some way by his sexual contact with her? Did he resent her for taking away his virginity? Did he begin to regard prostitutes as a danger to mankind, to be punished and made an example of?

We have already seen how Thompson, like de Quincey, carried two books around with him when he was living on the London streets, which he refused to sell, even though he must often have been starving, freezing in the open air and desperate for opium. These books were a volume of the poems of

William Blake, and another of plays by the ancient Greek playwright, Aeschylus. Apart from 'Tyger tyger burning bright' Blake's most famous line, about the harlot's cry, is contained in the following lines from his *Auguries of Innocence*:

> The whore and gambler, by the state
> Licensed, build that nation's fate.
> The harlot's cry from street to street
> Shall weave old England's winding-sheet.
> The winner's shout, the loser's curse,
> Dance before dead England's hearse.

Auguries is a strange, disturbing poem which insistently names things that are evil and states that, however insignificant they may seem, they cause more evil than we might suspect, by their very existence. Likewise, great evils in society are reflected in things like the sound of a gnat, or the poison of a snake. Earlier in the poem we learn that:

> A robin redbreast in a cage
> Puts all heaven in a rage.
> A dove-house fill'd with doves and pigeons
> Shudders hell thro' all its regions.
> A dog starv'd at his master's gate
> Predicts the ruin of the state.
> A horse misused upon the road
> Calls to heaven for human blood.

Can it be that Thompson's drug-addled brain learned

from Blake that something he personally did might save England, or save the world, or please heaven in some lasting, disproportionate, significant way?

The books a future poet chooses to take with him into the abyss must surely say something about the future poet, and certainly Blake's mysticism and eccentricity were reflected in Thompson's later poetic output. The same can be said of Thompson's relationship to the playwright Aeschylus, and if we believe that Thompson was indeed Jack the Ripper, then the influence of the Greek master can be seen as very dark and disturbing.

Aeschylus's most famous work is the Oresteia, a trilogy of plays based around the character of Orestes, an ancient prince of Greece. In the central play, Orestes murders his own mother, because she has murdered Orestes' father Agamemnon. In the last play, Orestes is chased by the Furies, terrifying personifications of human conscience and guilt.

The Oresteia's rich mix of murder, passion and guilt might have appealed to and even inspired Jack the Ripper, whoever he was, and we find Aeschylus in various forms in Thompson's poems. *The Hound of Heaven*, Thompson's best-known poem, relates how the poet is chased relentlessly by God, who will not slacken his pace – and in God's universe, we are constantly reminded in the poem, there is nowhere to hide from God.

Some have suggested that the headlong pursuit in *The Hound of Heaven* reflects the poet's desperate attempt to find his lost street-girl, but Orestes' pursuit by the Furies is certainly also there, though the pagan Greek idea is Christianised.

Indeed, in *Agamemnon*, the first play in the trilogy, the character Cassandra is described as a hound on the scent, and in *The Libation-Bearers* the Furies are described as hell-hounds.

We have already seen how, in *The Hound of Heaven*, Nature is described as a 'step-dame' who can offer no help to the soul fleeing God. We have also seen how Thompson may have transformed some unhealthy sense of revulsion against a woman, or women in general, into the grim 'Land of the Bare Shank-Bone' of his poem *The Nightmare of the Witch-Babies*. Here Thompson also includes the revolting idea of a witch-baby with its abdomen split open:

> And its paunch was rent
> Like a brasten [burst] drum;
> And the blubbered fat
> From its belly doth come
> With a sickening ooze – Hell made it so!

The image of the rent 'paunch' is horribly reminiscent of the photographs taken in 1888 of the naked dead body of Catherine Eddowes, the fourth of the five canonical victims, showing her abdominal wounds. Thompson's assertion that 'Hell' had caused the 'rent' in the baby's 'paunch' is also reminiscent of the letter sent, with what was supposed to be part of Eddowes' kidney, to George Lusk, head of the Whitechapel Vigilance Committee. Postmarked for October 15th 1888, the letter was signed 'catch me when you can mister

Lusk' and gave the address of origin as Hell itself.

Another feature of Thompson's *Witch Babies* poem that recalls a Ripper letter is the poet's use throughout of the phrases 'Ho! Ho' and 'Ha! Ha!'. The so-called 'Dear Boss' letter, sent to the Central News Agency in London in September 1888, uses 'ha ha' twice. This is the letter where the nick-name 'Jack the Ripper' was used for the first time. The 'Dear Boss' letter is also linked to Catherine Eddowes, because the author promises to clip an ear from his next victim, and part of one of Eddowes' ears was cut off.

There is a possible link back to Thompson's lost street-girl in verse two of the *Witch Babies* poem, where the poet describes the 'lusty knight' riding on 'the strand' of the Land of the Bare Shank-Bone. Readers will remember that the street-girl's regular 'pitch' was on the Strand. 'Strand' with a small 's' is of course a name for a beach or shore – did Thompson mean to suggest both?

One problem with finding traces of the Ripper murders in the *Witch Babies* poem is that if, as Walsh believes, Thompson dropped the poem through the letter-box of *Merry England* in February 1887, then it surely cannot reflect Thompson's memories of horrors he had committed, but only a Cassandra-like prediction of horrors he felt he might commit, if he really was the Ripper. And many other poets have used revolting imagery without any suspicion of their being serial killers, or even sexually perverted, attaching to them. The Elizabethan poet Edmund Spenser deployed disturbing imagery in his long allegorical poem *The*

Fairy Queen, and Spenser was a particular favourite of Thompson's, who called him 'the poet's poet' and talked up his influence on many other fine poets. Here is Spenser's description of the allegorical monster Error, with some of the typical Spenserian spelling modernised:

> Half like a serpent horribly displayed,
> But th'other half did woman's shape retain,
> Most loathsome, filthy, foul, and full of vile disdain.

> And as she lay upon the dirty ground,
> Her huge long tail her den all overspread,
> Yet was in knots and many boughtes [coils] upwound [twined],
> Pointed with mortal sting. Of her there bred
> A thousand young ones, which she daily fed,
> Sucking upon her poisonous dugs, each one
> Of sundry shapes, yet all ill favoured:
> Soon as that uncouth light upon them shone,
> Into her mouth they crept, and sudden all were gone.

Nothing in Thompson's writings adds up to a frank admission of his being Jack the Ripper, and, like many other popular Ripper suspects, there is nothing to connect Thompson directly to the crimes. Unlike some of the other Ripper suspects, Thompson did not seem to know anyone connected to the killings, and although Walsh suggests that he might have been questioned by the police at the time, there is no record of this. There is also no record of his having committed any violent crimes, and people who knew him remarked on his gentleness, placidity and even indolence.

As we have seen, Francis could be clumsy, dreamy, abstracted and absent-minded. He was physically weak, and when he tried to sign up as a soldier, attempts to build up his strength through exercise quickly failed. By contrast, it is thought that, at least at the time of the murders, Jack the Ripper would have needed to be quick, decisive, physically strong, and hyper-alert to the possibility of capture or discovery.

The first phase of Jack the Ripper's approach to his victims, if we set aside for a moment any advance planning, would have been his initial approach to his victims, when, particularly at the height of the Ripper scare, he would have needed to use his appearance, and reassuring language, to convince them that he was just a harmless potential customer. Ramshackle in appearance, and often tongue-tied and diffident in company, Thompson would surely have found this a challenge.

It is dangerous, of course, to argue against Thompson's Ripper candidacy on the basis of his personality as it exhibited itself in the civilised setting of the Meynells' dining-room. As Robert Louis Stevenson's story about Jekyll and Hyde made clear, it is possible for two or more contradictory personalities to reside in the same person, and explicit links were made between Hyde and the Ripper in 1888, when a theatrical version of the story was alarming audiences in London's West End. Although Jekyll effects his change with what amounts to a magic potion, it is easy to substitute alcohol or laudanum for his formula: both can cause mental changes, as can a disease which, it is now thought, Francis Thompson may have acquired during his time on the streets, carried into his new life as a celebrated writer, and possibly died from.

7. Blood and Brain

Although the shade of the poet Thomas Chatterton dissuaded Francis Thompson from suicide, and although the Meynells snatched him from the jaws of death on the streets in 1888, it seems that the poet's body never fully recovered from its privations after 1885, and he may also have lived out the rest of his life with permanent damage to his brain, caused by his years of malnutrition.

The ex-medical student diagnosed himself as a victim of beriberi, a condition caused by a lack of what we now know as vitamin B1, or thiamine. Although beriberi sounds like a tropical disease, readers in the UK will not have to go far to see sufferers from a mild form of beriberi. These can often be found in drinkers' pubs or bars – not the pubs where the millenials, the new yuppies, stand around drinking cocktails or craft lagers, nor the gastro-pubs where families can be seen at Sunday lunchtime wolfing down Yorkshire puddings, but the real drinkers' pubs, where middle-aged men will spend all day in a state of intoxication. Many of the features that make an alcoholic recognisable as such are symptoms of a form of beriberi, which is just one of the disadvantages of regular heavy drinking.

In her 1988 biography of Francis Thompson, Brigid Boardman used outside medical expertise to confirm that the poet was probably right to identify himself as a sufferer. Among other symptoms, patients with beriberi can experience weight loss, general weakness, confusion, clumsiness, a restricted ability to perceive the world via their senses, impaired speech and chaotic emotions.

Given the poor understanding of nutrition in late nineteenth century England (thiamine was not isolated until 1911) it is hardly surprising that, as seems likely, Thompson's failure to eat a balanced diet between 1885 and 1888 left him with lasting health problems. The death of his sweetheart Katie King in 1900 might also have sapped his will to live.

In his last years, Thompson resumed his opium habit, with the excuse that it relieved some of the symptoms of the illness that would ultimately kill him. He died in 1907, at the age of forty-seven. By a strange coincidence, this age is said to be the average life-expectancy of modern rough-sleepers on the streets of London.

Select Bibliography

Begg, Paul, Fido, Martin and Skinner, Keith: *The Complete Jack the Ripper A-Z*, John Blake, 2010

Begg, Paul: *Jack the Ripper: The Facts*, Robson, 2006

Bierce, Ambrose: *The Devil's Dictionary*, Dover, 1993

Boardman, Brigid M.: *Between Heaven and Charing Cross: The Life of Francis Thompson*, Yale University Press, 1988

Booth, William: *In Darkest England and the Way Out*, Charles Knight, 1970

Clerke, William M.: *The Secret Life of Wilkie Collins*, Ivan R. Dee, 2004

de Quincey, Thomas: *Confessions of an English Opium Eater and Other Writings*, Oxford, 2013

Evans, Stewart P and Skinner, Keith: *The Ultimate Jack the Ripper Sourcebook*, Robinson, 2001

Fowles, John: *The French Lieutenant's Woman*,

Triad Granada, 1981

Goodman, Ruth: *How to be a Victorian*, Penguin, 2014

Hopkins, R. Thurston: *Life and Death at the Old Bailey*, Herbert Jenkins, 1935

Jakubowski, Maxim and Braund, Nathan (eds.) *The Mammoth Book of Jack the Ripper*, Robinson, 2008

London, Jack: *The People of the Abyss*, Echo, 2007

Matthews, Rupert: *Jack the Ripper's Streets of Terror*, Arcturus, 2013

Meynell, Everard: *The Life of Francis Thompson*, Burns & Oates, 1913

Patterson, Richard: *Jack the Ripper: The Works of Francis Thompson*, Austin Macauley, 2017

Penzler, Otto: *Jack the Ripper*, Head of Zeus, 2016

Reid, J.C.: *Francis Thompson: Man and Poet*, Routledge and Kegan Paul, 1959

Rivett, Miriam and Whitehead, Mark: *Jack the Ripper*, Pocket Essentials, 2006

Rumbelow, Donald: *The Complete Jack the Ripper*, Virgin, 2016

Stevenson, Robert Louis, *Dr Jekyll and Mister*

Hyde, Wordsworth, 1993

Sugden, Philip: *The Complete History of Jack the Ripper*, Robinson, 2002

Thomas, Donald: *The Victorian Underworld*, John Murray, 1999

Thompson, Francis: *The Works of Francis Thompson, Volume 3: Prose*, Burns & Oates, 1913

Thompson, Francis: *Selected Poems*, Burns, Oates and Washbourne, 1908

Thompson, Francis: *Selected Poems*, Thomas Nelson, 1938

Thompson, Francis: Complete *Poems,* Waxkeep, 2015

Walsh, John: *Strange Harp, Strange Symphony: The Life of Francis Thompson*, W.H. Allen, 1968

Webb, Simon: *American Jack: Jack the Ripper and the United States*, Langley Press, 2017

Website: www.casebook.org

For free downloads and more from the Langley Press, please visit our website at:
http://tinyurl.com/lpdirect

Printed in Great Britain
by Amazon